student
WORKBOOK

GCSE History
USA, 1919–41

Nick Dyer & Geoff Layton

Philip Allan Updates, an imprint of Hodder Education, part of Hachette Livre UK, Market Place, Deddington, Oxfordshire OX15 0SE

Orders
Bookpoint Ltd, 130 Milton Park, Abingdon, Oxfordshire OX14 4SB
tel: 01235 827720, fax: 01235 400454
e-mail: uk.orders@bookpoint.co.uk
Lines are open 9.00 a.m.–5.00 p.m., Monday to Saturday, with a 24-hour message answering service. You can also order through the Philip Allan Updates website: www.philipallan.co.uk

© Philip Allan Updates 2008

ISBN 978-1-84489-141-2

Photograph of Franklin D. Roosevelt on the cover courtesy of TopFoto.

Printed in Spain

Hachette Livre UK's policy is to use papers that are natural, renewable and recyclable products and made from wood grown in sustainable forests. The logging and manufacturing processes are expected to conform to the environmental regulations of the country of origin.

Introduction

This workbook is designed to help you prepare for the USA option of your GCSE Modern World History course. It covers the requirements of the following examination boards:

- AQA: The USA, 1919–41
- OCR: The USA, 1919–41
- Edexcel: The USA, the Depression and the New Deal

The content is divided into seven topics, each of which provides an overview of an important aspect of US history from 1919 to 1941.

Each topic aims to:

- strengthen both your **knowledge** and **understanding** of the period
- test your ability to **explain** and **communicate** your response clearly and precisely
- help you develop your ability to **analyse** and **evaluate** sources

The notes in this workbook should be used in conjunction with your class notes and textbooks. This will enable you to provide comprehensive and effective answers that will be helpful when you come to revise for the exam.

The questions test your ability to:

- define terms and concepts
- use source material critically to answer questions
- complete a partially filled table
- write short-answer responses
- label diagrams and tables
- write extended answers, based on exam-type questions

Space is provided for your answers — the line allocation given to each question indicates how much you should be aiming to write for your answer. The final question in most topics gives you the opportunity for **extended writing** and should therefore be answered on separate sheets of paper.

Topic 1 American isolationism

Key question

Why did the USA retreat into a policy of isolation after the end of the First World War?

Key content

- Rejection of the peace treaty
- Why America refused to join the League of Nations
- Tariff policy — Fordney-McCumber Tariff of 1922
- Immigration controls — the quota system

The USA and the First World War

How did the USA react to the end of the First World War?

The US Constitution

The USA is a federal republic. This means that:

- It has no king or queen as its head of state.
- Power is divided between the federal government and the individual states, e.g. Virginia, Kentucky (see map on page 12).

In 1918, 48 states made up the USA. Each state can make its own laws on certain issues, such as education, while the federal government makes laws on issues of concern to all the states, such as foreign policy or defence.

The USA has a presidential system of democracy, which means that the three main branches of government are separated (see Figure 1) to ensure that no single branch or individual becomes too powerful.

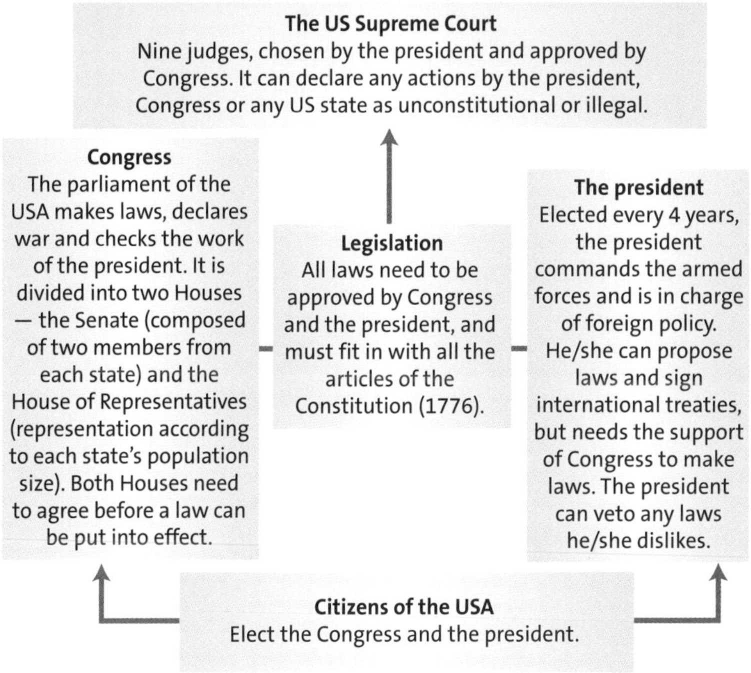

The US Supreme Court
Nine judges, chosen by the president and approved by Congress. It can declare any actions by the president, Congress or any US state as unconstitutional or illegal.

Congress
The parliament of the USA makes laws, declares war and checks the work of the president. It is divided into two Houses — the Senate (composed of two members from each state) and the House of Representatives (representation according to each state's population size). Both Houses need to agree before a law can be put into effect.

Legislation
All laws need to be approved by Congress and the president, and must fit in with all the articles of the Constitution (1776).

The president
Elected every 4 years, the president commands the armed forces and is in charge of foreign policy. He/she can propose laws and sign international treaties, but needs the support of Congress to make laws. The president can veto any laws he/she dislikes.

Citizens of the USA
Elect the Congress and the president.

Figure 1 The political system in the USA

The First World War began in Europe in 1914. At first, the USA remained officially neutral and did not join the conflict. This was partly because of its traditional policy of isolationism, but also because American public opinion was divided, due to the diverse European backgrounds of its citizens.

Democrat President Woodrow Wilson continued to preach peace in 1915–16, but by April 1917 the USA entered the war on the side of the Allied countries (Britain, France, Italy and Russia) for several key reasons:

- An increase of German submarine attacks on American ships.
- The British and French markets were more important than the German market. Indeed, sales to Britain and France soared from $825 million in 1914 to $3.2 billion in 1916.
- The USA could not afford to see Germany winning the war against countries such as Britain, which owed the USA large amounts of money.

With its powerful economy and financial strength, the USA helped bring about an end to the war. Over 1 million Americans fought on the Western Front in 1918, and, despite the defeat of Russia by Germany in early 1918, Germany surrendered to the Allies in November of that year.

Woodrow Wilson

The entry of the USA into the First World War ended decades of isolation, although many Americans still did not want to be involved in European squabbles. To combat this, Wilson made his famous 'Fourteen Points' speech in January 1918, proposing a clear set of war aims with the objective of establishing world peace. He presented the war as a struggle for freedom and democracy, and wanted the USA to take a leading global role through the creation of a League of Nations (the most important of his 14 points). The League of Nations was to be an association of nations with the main aim of preventing war and upholding peace by settling all international disputes through dialogue.

Despite Wilson's proposals, many Americans were horrified at the losses in the war and wanted US troops to withdraw from Europe. They wished to maintain the policy of isolation and were suspicious of the USA joining the League of Nations.

The domestic divisions in US politics were exacerbated after the Armistice of November 1918. Wilson attended the Paris peace conference in person, though he took with him fellow Democrats only. As a result, in his absence, the Republicans played on citizens' fears that Wilson would sign agreements binding the USA to the future of Europe, including possible future wars.

Political parties

American politics is dominated by two parties: the Democrats and the Republicans.

Democrats traditionally drew support from white people in the agricultural area of the 'Old South' in the USA, but increasingly attracted new immigrant groups in the north, such as the Irish, Jews and Italians. The trade unions also tended to support the Democrats. Although the Democratic Party supported capitalism (and private enterprise), it was prepared to let government intervene in everyday life in the interests of society.

Republicans received support mainly from the middle classes and businessmen, especially those of white Anglo-Saxon Protestant backgrounds in the northern states. Many African-Americans supported the Republicans, but tended to vote for the Democrats after 1933 following Roosevelt's New Deal (see Topics 6 and 7). The Republicans were strong supporters of capitalism in the 1920s and 1930s and opposed the state directing social and economic policies.

The major problem with President Wilson's political aims was that he required the support of Congress to make any agreements and commitments (see Figure 1 on page 3). In the 1918 elections, the Republican Party gained a majority of seats in both Houses. They were critical of Wilson's lack of consultation on the postwar peace treaties and, more specifically, his plans for the USA to join the League of Nations. The increased political influence of the Republicans reflected the general concern over Wilson's direction, and public opinion hardened against the president and his policies.

Isolationism

 How did the policies of the US government encourage isolation?

A series of events after the end of the First World War led the USA on a path of isolationism, during which time it concentrated on internal affairs.

The rejection of the Treaty of Versailles and the League of Nations

When the German government reluctantly signed the Treaty of Versailles, Wilson travelled around the USA in a campaign to persuade the American people and Congress to support the treaty and the League of Nations. However, in late September 1919 Wilson suffered a stroke and, although he remained in office, he was severely weakened and could not lead his campaign with the necessary energy.

In contrast, the isolationists, led by the Republicans, campaigned against the idea of the League. They presented it as an organisation that upheld British and French imperial power and was anti-German. Therefore, the Versailles Treaty was rejected in a Senate debate on 19 March 1920 — and as a result the USA never joined the League of Nations.

The election of President Harding

In 1920, the Republican Warren Harding was elected president. Harding glorified pre-war times, promising 'a return to normalcy' — the USA would focus on internal political and economic matters and withdraw from European affairs. He wanted a return to the USA's traditional values, with an emphasis on economic growth (see Topic 2).

The Fordney-McCumber Tariff Act

A tariff is a tax or duty levied on imported goods. It is intended to make goods from abroad (imports) more expensive than goods produced in the home country. Tariffs are a kind of economic protection for domestic agriculture and industry.

In the 1920s, Harding's Republican administration believed that the introduction of tariffs would lead to more economic growth in the USA. Therefore, it passed the Fordney-McCumber tariff in 1922, which placed duties on 28 goods coming into the USA. The tariffs raised taxes as high as 60% on wheat, corn and beef imports, as well as chemicals and textiles.

The Fordney-McCumber tariff reflected the American mood of isolationism of the 1920s, but it was short-sighted and selfish.

In fact, the tariff ultimately led to a decline in world trade, to the disadvantage of most nations (see Topic 4).

Immigration controls

Between 1900 and 1913, 13 million immigrants came to the USA, prompting concern over the extent of immigration. Many of these new immigrants were from southern and eastern Europe: Italy, Greece, Poland and Russia. Many were Catholics, with diverse cultural backgrounds. Others, not surprisingly, could not speak English on their arrival, so it was easy to accuse them of not being 'true Americans' and importing foreign ideas and values to America, such as socialism and communism. In contrast, many 'true Americans' were descendants of settlers from Protestant west European countries, such as Britain, Germany and Scandinavia. They were nicknamed 'WASPs' (white Anglo-Saxon Protestants).

American distrust of the new immigrants did not die down after the First World War. In fact, an increasingly powerful anti-immigration mood developed because of:
- the isolationist move to withdraw from international relations
- the exaggerated fears of communism in the wake of the Russian Revolution (see also the 'Red Scare' in Topic 3)

Congress passed the emergency Quota Act in May 1921. This limited immigration each year to 3% of the current population of that nationality in the USA, according to the 1910 census.

When the law was due to expire in 1924, Congress applied a further quota in the National Origins Immigration Act, which limited immigration from Europe in any one year to 2% of the current population of each nationality in the USA, according to the 1890 census.

This 1924 Act had such a dramatic effect that in 1929 only 150,000 immigrants were permitted to enter the USA. Significantly, the Act was also geared to favour immigrants from countries in northwest Europe.

Key question

Why did the USA retreat into a policy of isolation after the end of the First World War?

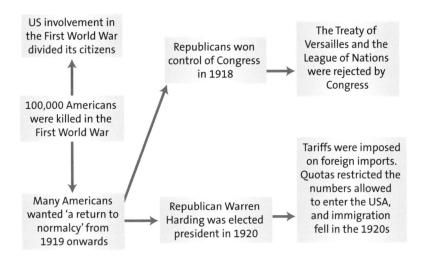

Figure 2 US isolationism in the 1920s

Questions

Use the information from pages 3–6, your class notes and textbooks to answer the following questions.

1 Define and explain what is meant by the following terms:
a The 'Fourteen Points'
b A federal state
c Tariff
d Quota Act 1921
e WASPs

1a

b

c

d

e

2 Complete the table by putting the following events in the correct chronological order and including the dates:
- The National Origins Immigration Act passed
- Harding elected as president
- Congress rejected the Versailles Treaty and the League of Nations
- President Wilson fell ill
- Republicans won control of Congress in elections
- USA entered the First World War
- The Fordney-McCumber Tariff Act passed

2

Date	Event
April 1917	
	The Fordney-McCumber Tariff Act passed

3 Explain in your own words how a federal law is passed in the USA.

4 a List two factors to explain the USA's decision to join the First World War.

b Give two reasons to explain the desire of Americans to see 'a return to normalcy' after the First World War.

3

4a

b

Questions

5 Complete the table, which analyses the development of US isolationism after 1919.

Development of isolationism	How and why did this occur?
Refusal to join the League of Nations	
Imposition of tariffs on imported goods	
Immigration controls	

6 Complete the table to highlight differences between the Democratic Party and the Republican Party in the early twentieth century.

6

	Democrats	Republicans
Who supported them?		
From which geographical areas did they draw support?		
What were their main economic aims?		
What were their main foreign policy aims?		

7 Read Source A. Explain what you can learn from the source about attitudes to immigrants in the USA in the 1920s.

Source A

For some years in the early twentieth century white Anglo-Saxon Protestant Americans had been feeling 'swamped' by non-Protestant immigrants with darker skins than their own, especially Catholics and Jews from Europe. An immigration law of 1921 established a national quota system, designed so that few people from eastern and southern Europe could get in.

H. Ward, *The USA, from Wilson to Nixon*, 1996

7

....

....

....

....

....

....

....

Questions

8 Study Source B.

a Why was this cartoon published in 1921? (Hint: what was happening in the USA in 1921?) In your answer, examine the purpose of the cartoonist. Use your own knowledge to help develop your answer.

b How useful is this source to a historian studying American immigration policy in the 1920s?

Extended writing

On separate paper, write a short essay in answer to the following question.

9 Explain the main reasons for US isolationism after the end of the First World War.

8a

b

Source B

THE ONLY WAY TO HANDLE IT.

 Key question

How far did the US economy boom in the 1920s?

Key content

- The expansion of the US economy in the 1920s — mass production in the car industry and consumer industries
- The consumer boom — hire-purchase and share ownership
- The fortunes of older industries
- The decline of agriculture
- Weaknesses in the US economy by the late 1920s

The American boom

? What was the basis of the economic boom of the 1920s?

Pre-war growth

Even before the First World War, the USA economy was growing quickly:

- The USA had an abundance of raw materials such as oil, coal, and iron, and it had a huge agricultural base (see Figure 1).
- The American population was growing rapidly, not only because of the increasing birthrate, but also because of the many immigrants who were attracted by the 'American Dream'.
- The USA's industries were growing. They were well-managed and modern, and they did not need to import many raw materials. As a result, there was an increasing demand for American goods domestically and for exports, particularly from trading nations such as Britain, Germany, Japan and countries within South America.
- American agriculture was very efficient compared with many peasant-based economies in Europe.

By 1914, the American economy had developed into one of the most powerful and modern in the world.

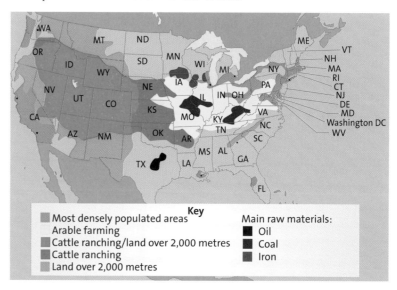

Figure 1 Map of USA showing raw materials, main centres of population and farming (2001)

Based on B. Walsh, *Modern World History* (2nd ed, John Murray)

The impact of the First World War

Because the USA stayed out of the First World War until 1917, its companies were able to take over markets supplied previously by other countries, while the economies of its European rivals were severely disrupted by the conflict. For example, the German chemicals industry led the world before 1914, but during and after the war the USA gained the dominant role.

During the war, America sold weapons and food to European countries, giving US businesses huge profits that were invested in developing new industries. By 1918, the USA was in a strong economic position and New York had emerged as the centre of world finance. In contrast, Britain and France were left deeply in debt from the costs of the war.

Government economic policies

In the nineteenth century, the USA generally supported the economic philosophy of laissez faire, in which it is believed that government should not interfere with the lives of the people — and that business should not be directed by government. In a way, this fitted in with the 'American Dream', which believed in the strength of the individual.

Although some Democrat presidents in the early twentieth century tried to limit the power of the major companies (trusts), the Republican presidents in the 1920s focused on policies to promote economic growth in the USA.

- They imposed tariffs on imported goods (see Topic 1) in order to protect US businesses from overseas competition.
- Taxation was kept as low as possible, enabling many people in the USA to buy more goods — mainly goods produced domestically.
- The trusts were given more freedom.

US presidents 1921–32

During the period 1921–32, the three US presidents were Republicans:
- Warren Harding (1921–23)
- Calvin Coolidge (1923–1928)
- Herbert Hoover (1929–1932)

They were conservative and believed in leaving industry and business free from government. Their political position was strong because the Republican Party dominated Congress during their time in office.

President Harding's government set the tone for the decade. Its policies reduced federal taxes, increased tariffs and imposed immigration restrictions. Harding was tainted with financial corruption and died suddenly in the summer of 1923. He was replaced with his vice-president, Coolidge.

Coolidge's period in office was marked by economic prosperity — he said famously that 'the business of America is business'. Coolidge did not stand for re-election.

Hoover took office in 1929 amid high hopes, claiming: 'We in America today are nearer to the final triumph over poverty than ever before in the history of any land'. Unfortunately, economic depression set in during the same year.

These policies built the foundations of the great American economic boom in the 1920s, which was supported by the development of new technological methods of production and a massive increase in consumer demand.

> **Government economic policies**
> In the 1920s, the Republicans enabled American business to thrive, and protected it from overseas competition by using tariff barriers.

> **The First World War**
> The war in Europe strengthened the US economy, further enabling the USA to increase its overseas trade. This generated huge profits to be invested in new industries.

> **Economic growth in the period before 1914**
> American industries and agriculture expanded vigorously. The growing population provided an increasing market for US goods.

Figure 2 The basis of the American economic boom

Industry

 Why did some industries prosper, while others did not?

Industry boomed in the 1920s — production virtually doubled and America's gross national product (GNP) grew from $78 billion to $103 billion. Output per worker improved by 43% between 1919 and 1929, and incomes increased by an average of 35%.

The USA had a range of well-established industries, such as coal and iron/steel. Other successful industries in the 1920s included chemical, electrical, film and those based on consumer goods in new technologies, such as telephones, radios, artificial fibres, vacuum cleaners and cars.

New, efficient methods of production made these goods cheap, and a mass market for them developed. In addition, the growing electrification programme meant that, in most urban areas at least, people could use the new electrical appliances in their homes.

The sale of consumer goods was supported by clever marketing:
- Sophisticated advertising encouraged Americans to spend their money.
- Hire-purchase offered people the chance to borrow money more easily — 60% of cars were purchased in this way.

The car industry

At the heart of this consumer boom was the expansion of the car industry. By 1929, more than 26 million cars were registered in the USA and during the 1920s approximately $1 billion a year was spent on the construction of main roads.

Henry Ford transformed the car industry when he pioneered mass production techniques. He first produced the Model T Ford in 1908. Production lines were set up in Detroit in 1913, and over 15 million cars were produced by 1925. This was achieved by the use of unskilled and semi-skilled labour, building small components of cars as they moved along assembly lines.

The car industry's expansion stimulated growth in other sectors of the US economy. For example:

- It created a huge demand for steel, rubber and glass.
- Roads had to be built — a road-building boom in the 1920s doubled the road mileage in the USA.
- New service facilities were created, and filling stations, garages and roadside restaurants sprang up across the nation. Motels, a word combining 'motor' and 'hotel', were set up to cater for the needs of motorists.
- Cars ran on petrol, so the oil industry boomed.

The impact of the Model T Ford

At first, the Model T Ford took 14 hours to assemble. By using mass production methods, Henry Ford reduced this to 1 hour 33 minutes, making it possible to produce 10,000 cars every 24 hours. Most significantly, this lowered the overall cost of the car, and its price fell from $1,000 to $360 between 1908 and 1916. This meant that by 1925, Ford represented 60% of America's total output of cars. Ford is said to have remarked: 'Americans can have any kind of car they want, and any colour they want, as long as it's a Ford, and as long as it's black.'

Not surprisingly, Ford was so successful in undercutting the price of other cars on the market that other companies soon introduced similar production methods, including General Motors in the USA and Morris in the UK.

Other industries copied the methods of the car industry in order to make more cheap mass-produced products. This stimulated further economic growth, and wages for ordinary workers in these industries increased, stimulating demand. Thus, the costs of consumer products fell and the average industrial worker's wage rose — fuelling a boom in demand for the consumer products.

However, not all industries did well in the 1920s:

- The coal industry faced competition from new forms of energy — oil, gas and electricity.
- Textiles depended on demand for clothes, and were hit hard by the changes in women's fashion for shorter skirts and dresses (see Topic 3). New synthetic materials such as rayon also became more popular, at the expense of the cotton and wool industry.

As a result, the wages of the workers in old industries did not flourish in the boom, and in 1929, 5% of the American workforce was unemployed.

The world economy in the 1920s

In contrast to the USA, most industrialised nations did not flourish economically in the 1920s and struggled to recover to pre-war levels:

- Britain had war debts, and at least one out of ten workers was unemployed. In 1929, whereas one out of five people in the USA owned a car, in Britain only one out of 43 were car owners.
- Germany had to pay large war debts and reparation payments, and in 1923 its currency was hit by hyperinflation.
- By the end of 1921, the Russian economy was in chaos and in the following decade its recovery was limited.

Agriculture

 Why did farmers not share in the prosperity of the 1920s?

American farming flourished in the decades before 1920, and was one of the largest sectors of the US economy, involving nearly half of working Americans. It became extremely efficient and introduced new fertilisers and machines, such as the combine harvester. During the First World War, American farmers successfully exported their food surpluses to Europe.

However, farming suffered in the 1920s for various reasons:
- European farmers started to produce again, and American farmers found it harder to find export markets for their goods.
- In response to America's tariffs (see Topic 1, page 5) many countries started placing tariffs on US agricultural imports.
- US farmers began to face stiff competition from Canada, which had cheaper food supplies.
- Most significantly, farmers continued to produce more food than could be consumed, driving prices down. Over-production may have been good for US consumers, but not for farm incomes. The decline in agricultural profits meant that many farmers had difficulty repaying the loans on their farms.

Table 1 Prices of wheat, corn and cotton

	1920	**1932**
Wheat (bushels)	$1.82	$0.38
Corn (bushels)	$0.61	$0.32
Cotton (pounds)	$0.16	$0.06

By 1929, many farmers had gone bankrupt (even before the Depression of the 1930s), and millions of unskilled farm workers faced unemployment. Not surprisingly, the impact of rural poverty forced the poor and desperate to migrate to the cities.

Winners and losers

 Did all Americans benefit from the boom?

Many Americans benefited from the prosperity of the 1920s:
- Unemployment fell from 11.9 million in 1921 to 1.9 million in 1926.
- The middle classes, skilled workers and big businesspeople benefited.
- The number of millionaires rose from 7,000 in 1914 to 35,000 in 1928.
- Many ordinary Americans owned consumer items previously only available to the rich.

However, for many Americans, the 1920s was a decade of poverty. The worst off included:
- farmers and farm workers
- African-Americans in the 'deep south' states, where many black people suffered poverty and racism
- unskilled 'new' immigrants in the big cities, such as Poles, Italians and Mexicans
- workers in the older industries
- women, who appeared to be more liberated (see Topic 3), but who were mostly poorly paid and employed in low-skilled jobs

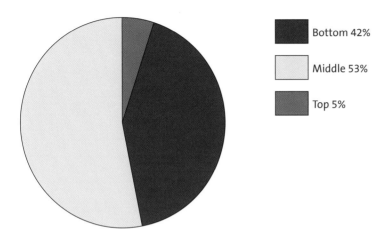

■	Bottom 42%
□	Middle 53%
▨	Top 5%

Figure 3 The distribution of wealth in the USA in the 1920s.

Poverty continued to be a feature of American society in the 1920s. It is estimated that 42% of Americans lived below the poverty line at that time.

In contrast, the boom benefited most the wealthiest few people. The richest 5% in America owned 32% of the nation's wealth, while the bottom 42% owned only 10%.

⚷ Key question

How far did the US economy boom in the 1920s?

The US economy continued to expand rapidly in the 1920s because of:

- the long-term strength of emerging America and the stimulus of the First World War
- the taxation and protection policies set up by the Republican governments
- the development of new technology and mass production, especially in the automobile industry
- hire-purchase and advertising, which allowed and encouraged people to purchase new gadgets
- shares — firms learned to raise money for expansion by selling shares on the stock exchange (this caused problems later)

The boom created great wealth opportunities and material advantages for some but, by the later 1920s, it also disguised a number of fundamental problems in the US economy. These problems are explained in Topic 4.

Use the information on pages 12–17, your class notes and textbooks to answer the following questions.

1 Explain the following terms and concepts:
a Trusts
b Consumer goods
c Synthetic materials
d Hire-purchase
e The 'tin Lizzie'

2 Which three factors helped develop the US economy during the First World War?

3 In 1925, President Coolidge is reported to have said that 'the business of America is business'. Explain what he meant by this.

1a

b

c

d

e

2

3

Questions

4 a In the table, tick the box in each row that is most appropriate to the status of US industries in the 1920s.

4a

Industry	Very successful	Successful	Struggling
Car			
Coal			
Electricity			
Leather			
Rayon			

b Choose one industry from the table in **4a** that was very successful in the 1920s and one that was struggling, and explain the reasons for their successes or difficulties.

b

Table 1

	1920	1929
Cars on road	9,000,000	26,000,000
Telephones	13,000,000	320,000,000
Radios in homes	60,000	10,000,000
Kilometres of built road	620,000	1,000,000

5 What can you learn from Table 1 about living standards in the USA in the 1920s?

5

6 The economic policy of the Republican governments in the 1920s can be described as laissez faire. Identify three features of laissez faire.

6

7 Why did the expansion of the car industry stimulate economic growth in many sectors of the US economy?

7

Questions

8 Study Source A.

a Identify the problems that US farmers faced during the 1920s.

b What is the message of the cartoon?

c How useful is the cartoon to a historian studying the position of US agriculture in the 1920s?

8a

b

c

Source A

An American cartoon showing an American farmer in the 1920s

PETER NEWARK'S AMERICAN PICTURES

Source B

In America the daily life of the majority is not unlike that enjoyed only by the very rich everywhere else. For instance, in 1925, 15 out of every 100 people had a telephone. In Europe only 2 out of every 100 had a telephone. 81% of all the motor cars in the world are to be found in the USA.

A French observer in America, writing in 1927, describing the prosperity of the 1920s

Source C

Not everyone did well during the boom years. Most of the profits made by industry went to businessmen and the owners of stocks and shares. Between 1923 and 1929 shares on average trebled in value. Farming slumped. During the 1920s six million people left the countryside to live in the cities, so that by 1930 over half the population lived in the hundred biggest cities.

A British historian, writing in 1987, commenting on the American prosperity of the 1920s

9 Read Sources B and C.

  a How is the content of the two sources different?

9a

  b Explain possible reasons why the interpretations in these two sources differ.

b

Questions

10 What economic divisions existed in the USA in the 1920s?

11 The points listed below were reasons for the 1920s boom in the American economy.

- The effects of the First World War
- Republican policies
- New methods of production

Which of these factors do you think was the most important? Explain your answer referring to *all* the points.

Key question

How far did US society change in the 1920s?

Key content

- Entertainment and the media — Hollywood and jazz
- The changing role of women — the vote, work, flappers
- Racism and discrimination — the Ku Klux Klan
- Prohibition and gangsterism — Al Capone

The image of the 'Roaring Twenties'

 What were the key features of the decade?

The 1920s was a period of great change in American society. It is often described as the 'Roaring Twenties' or 'the era of wonderful nonsense'. The decade was associated with changes in music, dance and fashion — a time of liberation and rejection of traditional values. However, not everyone was able to enjoy these changes.

Urbanisation

The effects of the 1920s were most evident in the expanding cities of the USA. Major cities, such as New York and Chicago, grew rapidly as more people moved to the suburbs and commuted to work. Skyscrapers, such as the Empire State Building, started to dominate the skyline, showing the self-confidence of the new American society. Shops and chain stores expanded, cinemas became a key source of entertainment, and bars and clubs developed.

However, for Americans living in rural areas, who had established beliefs in religion and the importance of the family, urban developments were a challenge to their values. They saw the 'big city' as the 'bad city' — it was dangerous and encouraged too much freedom.

Entertainment

With more leisure time and more money, the average American sought new entertainment in the 1920s.

By 1914, the American film industry had started to develop in the small Californian town of Los Angeles, in a place that became known as Hollywood. The climate was warm and sunny for most of the year, and Hollywood was near mountains and deserts — ideal for film locations. The film industry flourished, and by 1930 virtually every American town had a cinema. As a result, ordinary Americans were exposed to a different set of values, and began to copy the hairstyles, fashion and even lifestyles of the film stars.

Early films were 'silent', with stars including Charlie Chaplin, Douglas Fairbanks and Rudolf Valentino. However, the production of the first 'talkie' in 1927, *The Jazz Singer* with Al Jolson, offered a new experience and Hollywood was set to boom. By 1930, approximately 100 million cinema tickets were bought by Americans every week.

Film was not the only form of entertainment that developed in the 1920s. Sales of radios soared, generating a new audience for popular culture (see Topic 2). Many people began to listen to new music, such as jazz and blues. Traditionally, the appeal of jazz and blues was limited to black Americans in the South, but in the 1920s the music began to attract the interest of both black and white people in the cities. Such was its popularity that the 1920s became known as the 'Jazz Age'. Alongside the new music came new dances, such as the 'Charleston' and the 'Black Bottom'.

The decade also saw the beginning of mass attendance at sporting events. Big baseball games became popular and boxing events for famous fighters, such as Jack Dempsey, were in high demand.

Changing values

The 1920s was a decade of changing moral values. It witnessed dramatic changes in communication and the media through the development of film and radio. Features of the 1920s included:

- Hollywood films that played overtly on sexual images.
- The openly sexual nature of some songs and dances in jazz (which opponents described as 'the devil's music').
- The availability of contraception, and the increase of sex outside marriage.
- The increased availability of the car, which meant that younger Americans were able to escape the influence of their parents and create their own culture more easily. It also gave them the freedom to access other forms of entertainment, such as sports matches and the beach.

However, one should be careful not to exaggerate these trends. Some Americans expressed serious doubts about the appearance of more liberated women (see page 26) and many were scandalised by the new social developments. The older generation, and those in the rural areas especially, rejected the 'new values' of the 1920s.

Women

 How far did the role of women change during the 1920s?

The role of women changed significantly in the years after the First World War.

The vote

The right of women to vote became a key political issue before the First World War, and it had already been granted in some states; this was extended to all the states in 1920. However, few women were able to take an active role in politics, and in the Congress of 1928 only two female members were elected.

Work

Before the First World War, working women tended to be those employed in traditional 'female' areas, such as domestic service, clerical or secretarial work. Upper- and middle-class women were not expected to work — their traditional role was to look for a suitable husband and then to oversee the home and children.

During the war, women took on jobs in 'male' areas, such as the manufacturing industries, and this encouraged more women to abandon the traditional role of housewife. The changing attitudes in the 1920s were also encouraged by:

- the availability of the new electrical domestic goods, such as the vacuum cleaner and washing machine, which made domestic tasks easier
- the more liberal values demonstrated on the radio and in the cinema
- the economic expansion, which created many extra jobs

As a result, the number of women working increased by 25% during the decade, reaching 10.5 million by 1929. Typically, they worked in the new developing industries. Many middle-class women were drawn into some of the professional careers, especially teaching.

However, the majority of women carried on doing unpaid work in the home and on the land, and women's wages were a lot less than those of men.

Flappers

Before the war, upper- and middle-class women tended to lead traditional, conservative lives in terms of clothing, fashion and behaviour. They were not expected to smoke, to wear make-up or to take part in sport, and parents closely controlled all aspects of their relationships with men.

In the 1920s, there were clear signs of a changing mentality among women. Some women started smoking openly, drove cars, and took part in more sport. Others stopped wearing corsets and wore shorter skirts that revealed more flesh. As a further rejection of the traditional female image, hair was cut in a short bob. These women were nicknamed 'flappers'.

Most controversially, a few women started to lead their own social lives. They went out unchaperoned with men in public and took part in the new daring dances in the popular dance-halls. Evidence shows that there was much more sexual freedom for women outside marriage. However, the 'flappers' represented a small minority of mainly younger upper- and middle-class urban women living in the northern states.

Divorce

In the past, women in unhappy marriages had few choices open to them, but in the 1920s a new generation of women were no longer prepared to remain in failed relationships. The divorce rate more than doubled in the 1920s and this increase could be linked in part to the discontent of women within their marriages.

To sum up, the 1920s are often perceived to be a decade in which American women became more liberated. However, changes in fashion and behaviour that started among the younger and wealthier women in the cities spread only slowly to the rural areas and to other social groups. The evidence suggests that the majority of women in the 1920s were still housewives and remained traditional in their lifestyles and behaviour.

Indeed, many were outraged by what they saw happening in the cities among younger women.

Racism and discrimination

 How widespread was intolerance in US society?

Black America

Although slavery was ended with a proclamation in 1863, the majority of black Americans did not enjoy equal legal rights in the early twentieth century. They lived in poor conditions and were paid badly in unskilled jobs. Many of the southern states and cities segregated black and white people after the civil war, for example in education. In the 1920s, many southern states passed a range of new laws that extended segregation to public places such as taxis, buses and sporting events.

As a result, increasing numbers of black Americans migrated from the southern to the northern states, but they still tended to experience much poorer working and living conditions than white people, in areas such as housing, education and health services. Black Americans were generally not respected or welcomed by the new immigrants, such as the Poles and Italians, who saw them as a threat to their jobs.

However, there were increasing opportunities for black employment and education in the northern big cities, especially Chicago and New York, and the first black political organisations were created at this time:

- National Association for the Advancement of Colored People (NAACP) — founded by W. E. B. Du Bois and others in 1909.
- Universal Negro Improvement Association (UNIA) — founded by Marcus Garvey in 1914 in Jamaica.

Most significantly, black Americans were beginning to establish their own identity and culture out of the mood of the Jazz Age (see page 25).

Despite these positive developments, racism and discrimination remained a key feature of US society, and many horrific episodes of racial violence marred the 1920s.

The Ku Klux Klan

The Ku Klux Klan (KKK) was a racist movement, originally formed by white soldiers after the US Civil War (1861–65), and which declined gradually after its initial popularity. However, it was revived in 1915 by William J. Simmons, and it spread widely into the deep South and the Midwest.

The Ku Klux Klan was a frightening organisation, which believed in the supremacy of the white race. Its membership was open to white Anglo-Saxon Protestants (WASPs), with the aim of defending white superiority over black people and members of other ethnic and religious minorities, such as the new immigrants from south and east Europe.

Members of the KKK wore white gowns with pointed hats and masks, and they burned large crosses as symbols of their presence in an area. Their activities included secret ceremonies and, most disturbingly, they used terror and violence by assaulting their victims and burning property. Klan members also lynched hundreds of black people.

Between 1920 and 1925, 5 million Americans joined the organisation. The KKK attracted mainly poor unskilled white people, but powerful local officials including police officers, judges and politicians were also members. It is reckoned that in the 1920s, through sympathetic elected officials, the KKK controlled the governments of Tennessee, Indiana and Oklahoma.

The main reason for the collapse of the KKK in the late 1920s was a scandal involving David Stephenson, a 'Grand Dragon' (state leader), who was convicted of the rape and murder of a young secretary in 1925. There was a strong backlash against the KKK after the court case, but it also showed that the KKK had failed in its purpose to 'clean up' US society.

Table 1
Membership of the KKK

Year	Membership
1920	4,000,000
1924	6,000,000
1930	30,000
1970	2,000

The 'Red Scare'

America was traditionally seen as a country of democracy and free enterprise. However, some Americans in the 1920s felt an increasing threat to the US system from 'Reds' — people sympathetic to left-wing ideas such as communism, socialism and anarchism.

The reasons for the emerging 'Red Scare' among some Americans included:

- the Bolshevik revolution of 1917 in Russia, which seemed to confirm fears about the spread of communism

- the growing influence of trade unions, which stirred up a series of union-led strikes in 1919
- the large number of immigrants in the early twentieth century (see page 6), who were seen as possibly having 'Red' sympathies

The attitude of powerful and influential Americans was shown clearly by the leading industrialist Henry Ford, who feared that the activities of trade unions and socialist ideas would disturb his business and reduce his profits — although the 1920s was in fact a decade of economic growth.

In response to a number of terrorist-like bombings, the US government expanded the Department of Justice to spy on 'foreign radicals'. An extensive system of files on suspects was created (by J. Edgar Hoover, who later led the FBI) and some people were arrested and ordered to leave the USA. However, rumours of Red-inspired riots on 1 May 1920 came to nothing.

The famous case of two Italian anarchists, Nicola Sacco and Bartolomeo Vanzetti, illustrates the atmosphere of the time. They were tried in 1920 for robbery and murder, crimes which many people thought they did not commit. As a result, the political ideas of the defendants were investigated more during the trial than their alleged crimes. They were found guilty and sentenced to death, though many observers believed that the conviction was the result of prejudice against them as Italian immigrants and their radical political beliefs.

Immigrants and native Americans

Many Americans expressed concerns after the First World War about the number of immigrants, which led to the introduction of immigration quotas (see Topic 1).

Religious prejudices played a part in creating hostility between the older immigrant groups and the newer arrivals: the majority of Americans were Protestants, whereas the new immigrants were often Catholic or Jewish. Newer immigrants also tended to be poor and unskilled, often becoming involved in fights for better conditions that resulted in them being branded 'Reds'.

The number of Native Americans had declined significantly during the nineteenth century and the remainder were either moved into reservations or had given up their traditional ways of life altogether by the 1920s. Most lived in extreme poverty and were victims of racial discrimination. In response to widespread concern, they were granted US citizenship in 1924, and laws to improve the lives of Native Americans were passed in 1934.

Although many Americans saw their country as a 'melting pot' of different nationalities, races and religions, the 'Roaring Twenties' revealed some worrying signs of discrimination, prejudice and racism in the USA.

Prohibition

 Why was Prohibition introduced, and was it successful?

The Volstead Act

In the late nineteenth century, there was a growing movement to prohibit (ban) the sale of alcohol. This was led by two organisations: the Anti-Saloon League and the Women's Christian Temperance Movement. The movement enjoyed the strong support of the Protestant Churches and people in rural areas and by 1917 it had persuaded 18 of the states to become 'dry'. The campaign for Prohibition came to a head during the First World War. In December 1917, the Eighteenth Amendment to the US Constitution proposed banning the sale and distribution of alcohol. Eventually, in October 1919, the Volstead Act, which defined 'liquor' as any drink that contained at least 0.5% alcohol, became law and prohibited the manufacture, sale and consumption of liquor.

There were several reasons for banning alcohol:
- The **patriotic mood** — when America entered the war in 1917, many people agreed that it was wrong to enjoy alcohol while the country's young men were at war.
- **Religious beliefs** — for Christian believers, alcohol was seen as being against God's intention.
- **Social benefits** — e.g. no drunken fathers to ruin family life.
- **Practicalities** — leading businessmen and politicians argued that it would improve industrial production — especially to help the war effort.

Enforcement

Although several thousand federal agents were appointed (led by John Kramer, the first Prohibition Commissioner), it was difficult to enforce the law. The ban worked in some rural states, but in the cities, Prohibition simply created an enormous public demand for illegal alcohol. 'Speakeasies' appeared, supposedly selling soft drinks, which were really illegal bars serving alcohol behind the scenes. Other people set up their own stills to make 'moonshine'.

It was impossible to enforce Prohibition for several reasons:
- There were not enough Prohibition agents to enforce the ban

effectively across all states and cities. The size of the USA made it hard to control smuggling by 'bootleggers'.

- The police, who were low-paid, often turned a blind eye to the consumption, sale and smuggling of liquor.
- Those who were arrested often used bribery to escape conviction or were found not guilty by sympathetic juries.
- Prohibition led to a rise in crime and criminality, which made it even more difficult to enforce the law.

Corruption and gangsters

Prohibition gave criminals a chance to make a vast amount of money. Protection rackets and organised crime increased during the 1920s. In the cities, large and ruthless gangs

Al Capone and Bugsy Moran

The most infamous of the gangsters was Al Capone (nicknamed 'Scarface'), who controlled speakeasies, betting shops, gambling houses, brothels, horse tracks, nightclubs, distilleries and breweries in Chicago at a reported income of $100 million a year. He claimed that he was just a businessman, but from 1925 to 1930 he effectively dominated the city by controlling its politicians and officials. Capone was responsible for 500 gangland murders.

Throughout the 1920s, Capone battled with his main rival, Bugsy Moran, for the control of Chicago. This resulted in a notorious incident, the St Valentine's Day Massacre of February 1929, when Capone's men killed seven members of Moran's gang while Capone himself lay 'blamelessly' on a beach in Florida. Ironically, the authorities only managed to put Capone in prison in 1931 when he failed to pay his taxes.

emerged and expanded their control of the illegal trade in alcohol. They fought to dominate the speakeasies and the supply of bootleg alcohol, which was being smuggled into the USA from Canada. It has been estimated that gangsters made $2,000 million from the illegal making and selling of alcohol during Prohibition.

The growing degree of violence and corruption in Prohibition enforcement, particularly in Chicago and New York, shocked the nation and gave the impression that law and order was breaking down.

Repeal

Concerns about the consequences of Prohibition led to President Hoover calling for a government report, which was released in 1931 by the Wickersham Commission. Although it concluded that the Bureau of Prohibition Agency was inadequate and that Prohibition enforcement had broken down, it recommended more aggressive and extensive law enforcement measures, rather than the repeal of Prohibition.

However, in response to popular opinion, President Roosevelt, who was elected in 1932, passed the Twenty-First Amendment in February 1933, which repealed Prohibition once and for all.

Prohibition is generally seen as a political and social failure:

- The Prohibition laws were frequently ignored in the larger cities, and were flouted so much by so many that they were brought into disrepute.
- There was a huge increase in organised crime. The violence and corruption that emerged shocked many Americans.

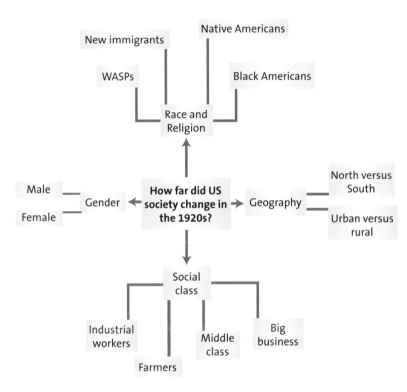

Figure 1 Factors affecting the lives of Americans in the 1920s

- The government lost money when it was no longer able to tax alcohol.
- Many people made their own alcohol.

However, it should still be remembered that:
- small towns and rural communities adhered to Prohibition
- there was a general fall in cases of alcoholism and fewer arrests for drunkenness
- alcohol consumption declined in the USA by 30%

🔑 Key question

How far did US society change in the 1920s?

It is extremely difficult to generalise about the extent of changes in the 1920s, so it is important to consider how factors affected the lives of Americans.

Use the information from pages 24–31, your class notes and textbooks to answer the following questions.

1 Explain the following terms and concepts:
  a Urbanisation
  b 'Talkies'
  c 'Reds'
  d 'Speakeasies'

2 a Why have the 1920s been called the 'Roaring Twenties'?

  b List some of the key features of the 'Roaring Twenties'.

3 Why did some people severely criticise the trend of urbanisation?

1a

b

c

d

2a

b

3

4 Complete the table opposite to identify changes that affected some women in the 1920s.

	Pre-war	1920s
Voting rights		
Work		
Clothes, make-up, smoking		
Relationships with men		
Divorce		

5 Why was the film industry in the USA so significant during the 1920s?

5

6 Study the picture of a flapper on page 26.
a Who were the flappers?

6a

b Why do you think the actions of flappers caused such a public stir in the 1920s?

b

Questions

Source A

There was never a time in American history when youth had such a special sense of importance as in the years after the First World War. There was a gulf between the generations. Young men who had fought in the trenches felt that they knew a reality their elders could not even imagine. Younger girls no longer consciously modelled themselves on their mothers, whose attitudes seemed irrelevant in the 1920s.

W. E. Leuchtenberg, *The Perils of Prosperity*, 1958

Source B

Though a few young upper-middle-class women in the cities talked about throwing off the older conventions — they were the flappers — most women stuck to the more traditional attitudes concerning 'their place'. Most concentrated on the home. Their daughters were likely to prepare for their roles as mothers and housewives. Millions of immigrant women and their daughters also clung to traditions that placed men firmly in control of the family.

J. T. Patterson, *America in the Twentieth Century*, 1988

7 Read Sources A and B.

a How does the content of Sources A and B differ?

7a

b Give possible reasons why the interpretations in Sources A and B are different.

b

8 a Explain what problems were faced by black people in America during the 1920s.

8a

....

....

....

....

....

b Were there any improvements to the lives of black people in the USA in the 1920s?

b

....

....

....

....

....

9 Give three reasons why some Americans joined the Ku Klux Klan in the 1920s.

9

....

....

....

....

....

10 Give three reasons why Prohibition was introduced in the USA in 1920.

10

....

....

....

....

....

Questions

Source C *Arrests for alcohol-related offences, 1920–25*	Year	Drunk	Drunk and disorderly conduct	Drunk drivers	Habitual drunkards	Total
	1920	14,313	6,097	0	33	20,443
	1923	45,226	8,076	645	177	54,124
	1925	51,361	5,522	820	814	58,517

Source: City of Philadelphia Police Department

11 Study Source C.

a What can you learn from Source C about Prohibition?

11a

b How useful is this source to a historian studying the effects of Prohibition in the 1920s? Remember to consider both the strengths and limitations of this source in your answer.

b

12 Explain why Prohibition led to an increase in criminal activity in the USA in the 1920s.

12

13 How useful is Source D in explaining why Prohibition failed?

13

Source D

AMERICAN SOCIAL HISTORY PRODUCTIONS

Extended writing

On separate paper, write a short essay in answer to the following question.

14 How far did American society change during the 1920s?

Topic 4 The Wall Street Crash

🔑 Key question

How far was speculation responsible for the Wall Street Crash?

🔑 Key content

- Problems of the 1920s — over-production, tariffs, unequal wealth
- Speculation
- The Wall Street Crash, October 1929

Long-term causes

❓ What were the long-term causes of the Wall Street Crash?

In the presidential election of November 1928, the optimism of the 1920s propelled another Republican to the White House. In March 1929, Herbert Hoover became the third successive Republican president of the USA. However, this optimism turned to despair when the stock market was hit by the 'Great Crash' in October 1929.

The crash was a crucial turning point in America's economic history, because it led to the Great Depression. It had a number of long-term causes, which can be traced throughout the course of the 'Roaring Twenties'.

Over-production

The unequal distribution of wealth in America meant that only a small number of people could afford the consumer goods available, and there were too few people to buy the volume of goods being produced. As a consequence, by the late 1920s the US economy was producing more goods than it could sell.

The boom of the 1920s was built upon selling consumer goods to rich and middle-class Americans. However, by the late 1920s, the market was running out of consumers for two main reasons. First, not all Americans benefited from the boom, including farmers, the unemployed and low wage earners. These people, who made up approximately half of all Americans, could not afford the consumer goods. Second, those people who could afford the goods had already bought what they needed — and many had borrowed money to do so, which left them in debt and unable to buy any more.

Tariffs

The spread of high tariffs had dramatic consequences. The USA could have exported its consumer goods, but many countries had economic problems after the First World War and could not afford US goods. Furthermore, when the USA introduced tariffs on imports, many countries responded by creating their own. This protectionism had a negative effect on US exports, as there was no outlet for the surplus American products.

Trusts

The Republicans allowed the development of trusts, which dominated industry. This allowed powerful individuals to work together to maximise their profits, keeping wages low and prices high. Over time, this depressed demand because people could no longer afford to buy the goods. By 1929, 50% of America's corporate wealth was controlled by 200 of its largest corporations. This concentration of wealth meant that in the event of these businesses failing, the country's economy would suffer.

Unstable banking

Despite the economic growth and the confidence of the 1920s, the American banking system was unstable, for two key reasons:

- The internal factor: the creation of economic wealth saw the establishment of many local banks. In the mid-1920s, banks were opening at the rate of five a day — but, worryingly, there was limited government regulation and even before the Depression two banks a day were closing.
- The world-wide factor: the First World War left many leading countries deeply indebted to the USA — especially the Allies and Germany. However, in the mid-1920s, the USA continued to give large loans to other countries on the basis that the world economy would continue to prosper.

The problems of America's unstable banking system were disguised by the prosperity of the 1920s.

By 1927–28 there were signs of an economic down-turn:

- Fewer new houses were being built.
- Sales of cars declined.
- Industrial workers' wages were no longer rising fast enough to buy all the consumer goods produced.
- Unemployment had already reached 4.2 million by 1928.

Stock market speculation

 How and why did Wall Street collapse in October 1929?

Between 1924 and 1929, the value of shares on the major stock market — Wall Street in New York — rose fourfold, and trading in stocks and shares became a popular form of speculation. (Such a confident time in trading is known as a 'bull market'; when prices fall it is known as a 'bear market'.)

There were a number of reasons for the Wall Street bull market in the 1920s:

- More savings. Many people were getting better wages and some used their surplus money to buy shares. Approximately 4 million Americans became shareowners and invested in order to profit from the rising shares. As a result, the increased demand for shares pushed their prices even higher and encouraged others to 'cash in' on the speculation.
- Rising dividends. The rise of share prices was a product of the boom and the confidence in the US economy in the 1920s. Many companies were making good profits (dividends) and the price of their shares rose in value too.
- Easy money. Interest rates were low, so people and banks were encouraged to join the stock market. This credit pushed share prices even higher and led to more speculation.
- Buying shares 'on the margin'. Many investors borrowed money to buy shares, in the belief that the rising share prices would allow them to sell their shares, pay back the borrowed money and still make a profit. These people were speculators.

They played on gaining a quick profit, and in the 1920s stock market speculation seemed like a certain bet, not a gamble.

By 1928, speculation was rife. Share prices continued to rise sharply, as millions of people scrambled to make easy money. By 3 September 1929, the stock market had reached an all-time high of 376.18 (Table 1 shows the average prices per year).

However, by late summer 1929, some investors were becoming nervous that prices were overvalued and a number of richer share-holders began to sell some of their shares while the going was still good. The market started to slow down gradually, and then collapsed suddenly on 'Black Thursday' (24 October 1929). Around 12,894,650 shares were sold and prices fell dramatically as sellers tried to find people willing to buy their shares.

On 29 October ('Black Tuesday'), over 16 million shares were sold as panic set in. The events of October 1929 became known as the Wall Street Crash, in which the market lost 47% of its value in 26 days. By 29 October share prices had plummeted to 212.33.

Table 1 The average of the highs and lows of the Dow Jones Index, 1922–32

Year	The Dow Jones Index
1921	63.9
1923	95.6
1925	137.2
1927	177.6
1929	290.0
1931	134.1
1932	79.4

🔑 Key question

How far was speculation responsible for the Wall Street Crash?

Although less than 1% of Americans possessed stocks and shares, the crash had an impact on the whole country (see Topic 5). Many sought 'scapegoats' and attributed the crash to the 'three Bs':

- bankers
- brokers (dealers in shares)
- businessmen

However, the speculation was not the fundamental cause of the crash and the Depression that followed. The 'bust' of October 1929 was the exaggerated reaction against the boom in shares, which had distracted the USA from its own fundamental economic weaknesses for several years.

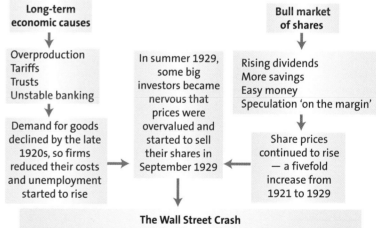

Figure 1 What caused the Wall Street Crash?

Use the information from pages 39–41, your class notes and textbooks to answer the following questions.

1 Explain the following terms and concepts:
a 'Bull' and 'bear' markets
b Buying shares 'on the margin'
c Interest rates
d The Dow Jones Index
e The 'three Bs'

2 Explain how each of the following long-term factors contributed to the Wall Street Crash:
a Over-production

b Tariffs

c Trusts

d Unstable banking

1a

b

c

d

e

2a

b

c

d

Questions

3 What signs were there of an economic down-turn in 1927–28?

3

....

....

....

....

4 Study Table 1 on page 41.

a Create a graph on the paper opposite from the data in Table 1. Highlight the high point of shares on 3 September 1929 using a different coloured pencil/pen.

4a

b Explain what you can learn from your graph.

b

....

....

....

....

5 Give three reasons why many Americans bought shares in the 1920s.

5

6 List three factors to explain why share prices continued to rise in the USA in the 1920s.

6

Questions

Source A

The rich man's chauffeur drove with his ears laid back to catch the news of the latest share prices. The window cleaner watched the ticker tape because he was thinking of using his hard-earned savings to buy shares. A financial reporter once told of a stockbroker's servant who made nearly a quarter of a million dollars profit, by buying shares 'on the margin'.

J. Vick, *Modern America*, 1991

7 Read Source A, in which an American author describes the stock market speculation of 1929. How useful is this source to a historian studying American attitudes towards stock market shares in the 1920s? Use the source and your own knowledge to develop your answer.

7

8 Why were share prices in the USA over-valued by 1929?

8

Extended writing

On separate paper, write a short essay in answer to the following question. (Include causes, contributions to the crash and links to other factors.)

9 'The most important cause of the Wall Street Crash was stock market speculation.' Do you agree with this statement?

Complete the table opposite to plan your answer.

Cause	Contribution to the crash	Link to other factors
Stock market speculation		
Conclusion		

The economic crisis in the USA

What was the impact of the crash on the US economy?

Financial collapse

Those who had invested heavily in shares, mainly the rich, lost the most and many were ruined. Ordinary Americans who had bought shares 'on the margin' with worthless share certificates also lost money. Many were made bankrupt, as they were unable to sell their shares and pay back what they had borrowed.

Many of the smaller US banks were ruined because they had lent out more money than they had on deposit, and people were unable to repay their loans. Those who had saved money during the 1920s were also ruined, as their money was lost when banks collapsed. Between 1929 and 1933, 5,000 banks closed down and the entire American banking system came close to collapse.

In December 1930, the leading bank in New York, the Bank of the United States, went bankrupt, and a series of European banks collapsed in the summer of 1931. As panic set in, people began to withdraw their money, leading to $1 billion being removed from US banks.

The failure of the world banking system turned the financial crisis into an economic disaster. From that moment, people not only lost faith in shares, but they also no longer trusted the banks.

The world economic depression

America was not alone in the Great Depression. It struck many of the industrialised nations of the world, including Germany, the UK and France (though not the USSR). World trade declined sharply, and by 1932 there were 12 million unemployed people in the USA, 6 million in Germany and 3 million in the UK. Prices fell even more sharply, adding to the decline in farming. The economic depression lasted into the 1930s and millions suffered great hardship.

The economic impact

The financial crisis led to the emergence of an economic depression (a sustained period of economic recession) that was characterised by:
- rising unemployment
- a lack of orders for manufactured goods
- falling prices

Demand for goods in the USA fell sharply. Many people and banks had lost money in the crash, which forced companies to reduce costs and lower production. As a result, workers were made unemployed, which further reduced demand (the cycle of economic depression).

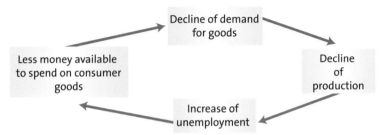

Figure 1 The cycle of economic depression

Even the people who had money and employment chose to spend less because confidence in the economy had collapsed. In response, businesses cut back production further and started to lay off more workers.

By the winter of early 1933 — the low-point of the Depression — it is reckoned that:

- industrial production had fallen by 40%
- farm income had fallen by 50%
- 32,000 businesses had failed
- wages had fallen by 60%
- share prices had fallen by 80%
- 12 million Americans were unemployed — one quarter of the workforce
- house-building had fallen by 80%

The economic effects were catastrophic. From its high point in the 1920s, the USA sank to a low. The Depression was more severe and lasted longer in the USA than in any other industrialised country.

Poverty and hardship

 What were the social consequences of the Great Depression in the USA?

The social impact of the Depression meant great hardship for millions of Americans. This was not only because of the severity of the economic decline, but also because very few states had any form of social welfare programme. This reflected America's laissez-faire attitude and its tradition of individual self-help.

Unemployment

The growing long-term unemployment was much higher than the national average in America's large cities because of the decline in industrial production. The black population was affected much more severely than the white population.

As a result, without any government welfare available, many people lost their homes. Shanty towns grew up around many of America's towns and cities, built out of any discarded material, such as cardboard and odd bits of wood. These were sad and depressing places, and they soon became nicknamed 'Hoovervilles' after the president, whom many blamed for their situation.

Without any income, the unemployed and homeless were forced to queue for handouts from private charity organisations at 'soup kitchens'. Belonging to a generation of Americans filled with pride, many felt ashamed at their new situation. Their despair was reflected in the increasing number of:

- suicides
- family break-ups
- mental illness cases
- high school dropout rates

Rural poverty

American farmers were already struggling economically in the mid-1920s (see Topic 2, page 16). During the Depression, things became considerably worse.

Many people were already in debt, with large mortgages to pay for machinery and land. When the price of agricultural produce fell sharply, for many farmers it was not worth producing crops or taking animals to market. This meant that they could not meet their mortgage repayments and had to sell their farms.

To make matters worse, a drought in the Midwest and South in 1931–32 led to soil erosion on the over-cropped farms. This created the 'dust bowl', an area in which the topsoil was blown away, making it impossible to farm.

Farmers faced a dilemma: stay on the land and make the best of a difficult situation, or pack up and leave their homes and land in order to find alternative work.

Some farmers headed for California in the hope of finding jobs, but they found little work and much hardship. These people were known as 'Okies', named after migrants from Oklahoma. However, the actual migration rate from rural to urban areas in the 1930s was lower than in the 1920s. The majority remained and suffered from rural poverty. They could not make a profit selling their products, but at least they could still eat, whereas the cities could no longer provide jobs.

The political effects of the Depression

 Why did Roosevelt win the 1932 presidential election?

Hoover's presidency

The blame for the Great Depression cannot be placed on Hoover — he was simply in the wrong place at the wrong time. However, contemporaries and historians have criticised Hoover for dealing with the effects of the Depression inadequately.

Hoover was a product of Republican economic policies, and he continued to advocate self-help and oppose state intervention throughout the Depression. He believed that the economy would correct itself and that 'prosperity was just around the corner'. He could not accept that there were major weaknesses in the US economy — if anything, he tended to put the blame on Europe.

Hoover's measures

For the unemployed and poor farmers, Hoover came to be seen as a 'do nothing' president. This was a little unfair, because he introduced a number of initiatives in an attempt to restart the economy:

- He cut taxes by $130 million in 1930 to give people more money, in order to increase demand in the economy.
- In 1931, he gave money to build large river dams, such as the Hoover Dam, to help create jobs.

- He cancelled war debts and reparations in the hope of expanding world trade.
- He established the Reconstruction Finance Corporation in January 1932 to provide $2 billion for struggling banks and businesses.
- In July 1932, the Emergency Relief and Construction Act was passed, which gave direct federal aid to the unemployed.

Hoover tried to persuade business leaders *not* to cut wages, and he supported more protection of the US economy by introducing the Hawley-Smoot Tariff Act 1930. However, the Act made matters worse, causing international trade to decline further.

Hoover's measures were ineffective, and between 1930 and 1932 the problems of the Depression increased. Hoover and the majority of the Congress were determined to keep the budget balanced between the government's expenditure and income (taxes). Therefore, their proposals were timid and did not provide federal relief to farmers and to the urban unemployed — they saw this as the responsibility of the states. As one historian has said: 'It was not that President Hoover did nothing, but that what he did was too little, and it came too late.'

The 'Bonus Army'

Hoover's handling of events gave the impression that he did not care about the suffering of Americans. 'Hoovervilles' and the 'Hoover blankets' (newspapers used as blankets) were mocking terms, and for many people, the treatment of the 'Bonus Army' confirmed Hoover's reputation as uncaring.

In June 1932, thousands of ex-servicemen of the First World War marched to Washington to ask for earlier payment of their war pensions. The 'Bonus Army' settled into a shanty town of approximately 30,000 protesters near the White House. Congress refused to pay the bonus, and on 28 July 1932, US troops — under the command of General Douglas MacArthur — broke up the protest with tear gas. Two protesters were killed and several hundred were injured. Although Hoover had ordered MacArthur to deter the Bonus Army with sensitivity, the incident caused people to see him as unsympathetic and callous.

The 1932 presidential election

The 'Bonus Army' incident occurred during the campaign for the presidential election of November 1932. Despite the country's ongoing economic problems, the Republican Party nominated Herbert Hoover as its candidate once again. The Democratic Party nominated Franklin D. Roosevelt, who had been governor of New York since 1928.

Hoover's campaign did not go well:
- He was a poor public speaker and failed to offer answers to the problems of the Depression.
- He continued to blame foreign bankers for the crisis and repeated his unfounded opinion that things would soon improve.
- 1932 coincided with the deepest point of the Depression.
- Hoover's name became associated with the worst aspects of the Depression, and his treatment of the 'Bonus Army' only made matters worse.
- He continued to support Prohibition, despite its problems.

The emergence of Franklin D. Roosevelt

Franklin D. Roosevelt was a cousin of Theodore Roosevelt (president 1901–09) and came from a privileged background. Although permanently disabled by polio in 1921, he was not deterred from his political ambitions in the Democratic Party. In 1928, he was elected governor of New York State.

When the Depression set in, Roosevelt set up an Emergency Relief Commission in New York to help the unemployed and homeless . His own disability gave him an insight into the problems of ordinary people and his words gave hope to many devastated Americans:

> I pledge you, I pledge myself, to a New Deal for the American people...
> This is more than a political campaign; it is a call to arms. Give me your help, not to win votes alone, but to win this crusade to restore America to its own people.

In contrast, Roosevelt's election campaign was very effective:

- Despite his physical limitations, he was a powerful speaker and he sold his new vision to America on a nationwide tour.
- He offered America a 'New Deal'.
- Although vague with his exact plans and policies, his approach offered hope to millions.
- Roosevelt was a 'wet' and supported the repeal of Prohibition.

Roosevelt won a landslide victory, with 57.4% of the total votes (7 million more than Hoover).

The 1932 election was a significant turning point in US history. Not only did Roosevelt become president, but the Democratic Party won control of both Houses of the US Congress and many state governorships. When Roosevelt took up the office of president in March 1933, he had the political power to confront the problems of the Great Depression.

🔑 Key question

What were the effects of the Great Depression?

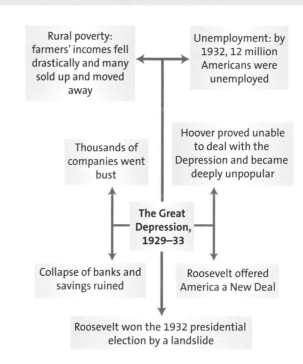

Figure 2 The effects of the Great Depression

Use the information from pages 47–51, your class notes and textbooks to answer the following questions.

1 Explain the following terms and concepts:
　a The 'dust bowl'
　b 'Hoovervilles'
　c 'Okies'
　d The 'Bonus Army'
　e Hawley-Smoot Tariff Act

2 Complete the table to summarise the main consequences of the Depression. Include at least three examples in each box.

1a

b

c

d

e

2

	The consequences of the Depression in America
Economic impact	
Social impact	
Political impact	

Questions

Source A

City	Black people as % of population	Black people as % of total unemployed
Chicago	4	16
Philadelphia	7	25
Pittsburgh	8	38
Memphis	38	75

3 Study the information in Source A. What can you learn from this source about how black Americans were affected by the Depression?

4 a Why was Hoover labelled a 'do-nothing president'?

b To what extent is this label fair?

3

4a

b

5 Look at Source B.

  a What can you learn from this source about the effects of the Depression on Americans?

  b How would this photograph have affected Hoover's election campaign of 1932?

5a

b

Source B

Source C

During his presidential term Hoover was to act incessantly, doing more than any other previous president had done in any previous economic crisis.

H. Brogan, *The Longman History of the United States*, 1999

Source D

Never before in this country has a government fallen to so low a place in popular estimation or been so universally an object of cynical contempt. Never before has a president given his name so freely to latrines and offal dumps, or had his face banished from the cinema screen to avoid the hoots and jeers of children.

An American political commentator, speaking after the election of 1932

6 Read Sources C and D.

a How does the content of these two sources differ?

b Explain possible reasons why the two interpretations are different.

6a

b

7 How did Hoover's treatment of the 'Bonus Army' help Roosevelt's election campaign?

7

....

....

....

....

....

....

....

....

8 In the table, list the main reasons why Roosevelt won the 1932 election.

8

Roosevelt's appeal	Hoover's problems

Questions

Source E

Millions of our citizens cherish the hope that their old standards of living have not gone forever. Those millions shall not hope in vain. I pledge you, I pledge myself, to a New Deal for the American people.

An election speech by Roosevelt, 1932

9 Read Source E. Do you think this was an effective campaign speech?

10 Study Source F. Which party do you think published this poster — the Democrats or the Republicans? Explain your answer by considering the purpose of this source. Use your own knowledge to develop your answer.

Extended writing

On separate paper, write a short essay answering the following question:

11 Explain why Roosevelt won the November 1932 presidential election.

9

10

Source F

Smile away the Depression!

Smile us into Prosperity!
wear a
SMILETTE!

This wonderful little gadget will solve the problems of the Nation!

APPLY NOW AT YOUR CHAMBER OF COMMERCE OR THE REPUBLICAN NATIONAL COMMITTEE

WARNING—Do not risk Federal arrest by looking glum!

PETER NEWARK'S AMERICAN PICTURES

Topic 6 The New Deal

 Key question

What measures did Roosevelt introduce to deal with the Depression?

Key content

- Roosevelt's inauguration and the '100 days'; the 'fireside chats'
- The banking crisis
- New Deal legislation; the alphabet agencies and their work

This is the first of two topics that consider the nature and impact of Roosevelt's New Deal, from 1933 to 1941. This topic examines the legislation of the New Deal, and Topic 7 considers the extent of its success.

The first New Deal

 What were Roosevelt's aims?

Roosevelt's inauguration

On 4 March 1933, Franklin D. Roosevelt was sworn in as president of the USA, having won a large personal mandate to tackle the problems of the Depression. Roosevelt's party, the Democrats, also took control of both Houses of Congress, so he had strong support.

The Beer Act, March 1933

During the election campaign, Roosevelt promised to end Prohibition. When he became president, he passed the Beer Act, which raised the level of alcohol permitted by the Volstead Act. At the end of 1933, Prohibition was repealed entirely.

This brought an end to the national controversy of enforcing Prohibition, but still gave individual states the right to limit alcohol if they wished.

Roosevelt's election campaign indicated that he was willing to use the power of federal government to pull America out of the Depression, which generated an expectation of change among the American public. Roosevelt's greatest immediate challenge was to restore America to a sense of confidence in the nation and the economy.

Roosevelt used his inauguration speech to generate a more positive mood. First, he reassured the American people that 'the only thing we have to fear is fear itself — nameless, unreasoning, unjustified terror'. Second, he tried to convey a more dynamic attitude by saying that 'this nation asks for action and action now'.

Roosevelt's priorities were:
- to restore confidence in the banking system, thereby encouraging Americans to save
- to help industry, business and farming to recover
- to cut unemployment

- to provide relief to those who were hit hardest by the events of the Depression

Many commentators recognised the new mood in America that greeted Roosevelt's inauguration, and expectations were high as he began to fulfil his election promises.

Roosevelt's first 100 days

 What measures did Roosevelt introduce to deal with the Depression?

The first 100 days of Roosevelt's presidency were marked by a flurry of activity. Roosevelt built upon and developed the work carried out under Hoover, but he also went much further. His main aim was to show Americans that something was being done to help them.

One of the most pressing problems facing America was the collapse of confidence in the US banking system since 1929. Americans had seen so many banks go bankrupt that they no longer saved their money in them. This meant that there was not enough money available for borrowing and investment.

A day after his inaugural speech, Roosevelt passed the **Emergency Banking Relief Act**, closing all banks as a national holiday from 6–9 March. Government officials were sent to check all banks and put them under federal control. Banks that were run badly were not allowed to reopen, but the

banks considered to be financially sound were allowed to restart under licence. After a few days, 5,000 banks were permitted to reopen with the promise of financial support from the government if necessary. This was endorsed by the Glass-Steagall Banking Act, which created the Federal Deposit Insurance Corporation (FDIC).

Roosevelt's 'fireside chats'

Roosevelt restored hope through his 'fireside chats'. From the start of his presidency, he addressed the nation through the relatively new medium of radio, and the chats soon became an established weekly feature. In this way, he explained his plans and helped restore the trust between the American people and their elected leaders — trust in America itself.

This dramatic action served to restore confidence in the US banking system and people began to trust their banks. An adviser to Roosevelt noted that this action 'marked the revival of hope'.

Measures to tackle the human problems of the Depression followed quickly. Roosevelt and his government were supported by a team of advisers (who became known as the 'Brains Trust' because many were former university lecturers), and they developed a range of agencies during the first 100 days. The main proposals are summarised in Table 1 on page 60 and demonstrate Roosevelt's idea of kick-starting economic growth through federal government investment. This became known as 'priming the pump'.

Table 1 The alphabet agencies

Agency	Aim	Summary of assistance provided
Federal Emergency Relief Administration (FERA) (May 1933)	To provide immediate emergency relief to the poorest	It gave $500 million to the states, which were spent on soup kitchens, blankets, free nursery schools for children and the creation of jobs.
Civilian Conservation Corps (CCC) (31 March 1933)	To create jobs for the unemployed	Camps were set up and organised by the army, giving young people work for 6 months in the countryside. Two million young men and 8,000 women took part in the 1930s. They were fed and paid 1 dollar a day. They planted trees on lands stripped of timber, created fences, and built canals and roads through forests.
Agricultural Adjustment Administration (AAA) (12 May 1933)	To boost farmers' income	It gave money to buy new machinery and fertilisers, and to provide help with mortgages in cases of severe distress. The main means of support was the use of quotas in each area to reduce agricultural production. This drove up prices and gave farmers higher returns for their produce. By 1936, farm incomes had risen by 50%, but the modernisation of farms led to more agricultural labourers losing jobs and leaving the land.
National Industrial Recovery Act (NIRA) (18 June 1933) Established two organisations		
Public Works Administration (PWA)	To create jobs for the unemployed	This agency, led by Harold Ickes, spent $3.3 billion on providing employment on large-scale building projects. It arranged for the building of flats in slum areas, schools, city halls, sewers, hospitals, roads, bridges, airports and naval vessels.
National Recovery Administration (NRA)	To improve working conditions in industries.	It was created to make employers and workers agree on fair prices, wages and working hours in the main industries. Membership of the NRA was voluntary, but firms following its rules could use the Blue Eagle badge of the organisation. Two million employers joined the scheme, affecting over 22 million workers. However, many businesses refused to join, and some who did join violated the codes of practice. Child labour was banned.

The Tennessee River valley suffered from natural problems that led to erosion:
- regular flooding in the wet season
- poor irrigation in the dry months

The farmers there were particularly poor, partly because the area crossed seven state boundaries and it was difficult for any individual state to take responsibility to resolve the problems. There was also little electricity provision in the area.

The TVA was established by Roosevelt in May 1933 to administer the area. Dams were built on the river to generate electricity by hydroelectric power (HEP), to control the floods and to irrigate the land. It led to the development of new industries such as paper-making and aluminium smelting, which created thousands of jobs.

The 'alphabet agencies' initiated in the first 100 days of Roosevelt's presidency were criticised by some who said Roosevelt did not do enough. Others claimed that he was interfering too much in America's traditional political and economic values. Nevertheless, the results of the first New Deal (which ran from March 1933 to November 1934) had tremendous results:
- It restored some confidence in government.
- It provided millions of new jobs.
- It gave relief from the worst aspects of mass poverty.
- It encouraged others to spend in order to create further growth and employment (see Topic 7).

The second New Deal

 How far did the character of the New Deal change after 1933?

The second New Deal (1935–36) began in the wake of the mid-term congressional elections in November 1934, in which the Democrats won an even greater majority than in 1932. Many new Democratic Party members wanted Roosevelt to go further and to pass more fundamental reforms of society to help the poor, the unemployed and working people.

Roosevelt was tempted to pass these radical reforms, partly to prevent Americans from being seduced into supporting more extreme alternatives, such as communism and fascism. In June 1935, Roosevelt presented Congress with a huge range of measures, which became known as the second New Deal. Whereas the first New Deal aimed to offer relief from the symptoms of economic collapse, the second New Deal aimed to reform the nature of American society. The main measures of the second New Deal are summarised in Table 2 on page 62. Although the New Deals had many opponents and unemployment remained stubbornly high throughout the 1930s in the USA, Roosevelt's work with the New Deal represented hope and action. For millions of Americans, these new agencies offered relief from the risk of starvation and the chance to escape from long-term mass unemployment. It represented a new American approach to dealing with social problems.

🔑 *Key question*

What measures did Roosevelt introduce to deal with the Depression?

Table 2 The second New Deal

Action	Purpose	Summary of assistance provided
Wagner Act, 5 July 1935	To improve workers' rights	It forced all employers to allow trade unions to operate in their businesses and to let them negotiate for better pay and conditions. Employers were prevented from victimising union members.
Social Security Act, 14 August 1935	To provide better welfare	It began a basic system of welfare by establishing a national system of old-age pensions, unemployment benefit and sick pay for most employees.
Works Progress Administration (WPA), 6 May 1935	To tackle unemployment	It provided work for approximately 3 million unemployed. Although the pay was low and some of the projects were of limited value, the WPA pumped over $11 billion into the economy by building hospitals, schools etc. The WPA also employed writers, artists and photographers in its various agencies (Federal Theatre Project, Federal Writers' Project, Federal Art Project).
Resettlement Administration (RA), 30 April 1935	To combat rural poverty	This aimed to give poverty-stricken farmers a new start on good land. It planned to resettle 500,000 families, but only resettled 5,000. It was replaced by the Farm Security Administration in 1937, which granted long-term, low-interest loans to enable poor farmers to buy family-sized holdings, and which also set up clean, well-run camps for migrant workers and their families.

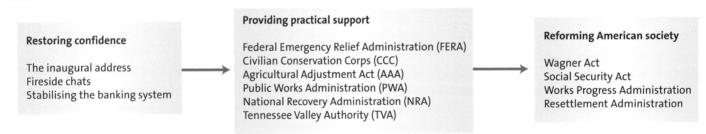

Restoring confidence

The inaugural address
Fireside chats
Stabilising the banking system

Providing practical support

Federal Emergency Relief Administration (FERA)
Civilian Conservation Corps (CCC)
Agricultural Adjustment Act (AAA)
Public Works Administration (PWA)
National Recovery Administration (NRA)
Tennessee Valley Authority (TVA)

Reforming American society

Wagner Act
Social Security Act
Works Progress Administration
Resettlement Administration

Figure 1 Roosevelt's response to the Depression

Questions

Use the information on pages 58–62, your class notes and textbooks to answer the following questions.

1 Explain the following terms and concepts:
  a The first 100 days
  b 'Fireside chats'
  c The 'Brains Trust'
  d The 'alphabet agencies'
  e The TVA

2 What did Roosevelt mean by 'priming the pump'?

3 What were the four main aims of Roosevelt's New Deal?

1a

b

c

d

e

2

3

4 Explain the measures taken by Roosevelt to restore confidence in the US banking system.

5 Read Source A. How accurate is this view of the importance of the bank rescue of 1933?

6 Study Source B. How useful is this cartoon to a historian studying Roosevelt's New Deal?

Source B

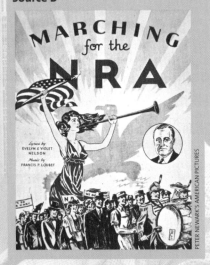

MARCHING for the NRA

Lyrics by EVELYN & VIOLET NELSON
Music by FRANCIS P. LOUBET

PETER NEWARK'S AMERICAN PICTURES

4

5

6

Source A

The bank rescue of 1933 was probably the turning point of the Depression. When people were able to survive the shock of having all banks closed, and then see the banks reopen again, with their money protected, there began to be confidence. Good times were coming up again. It marked the revival of hope.

R. Moley, an adviser to Roosevelt

Questions

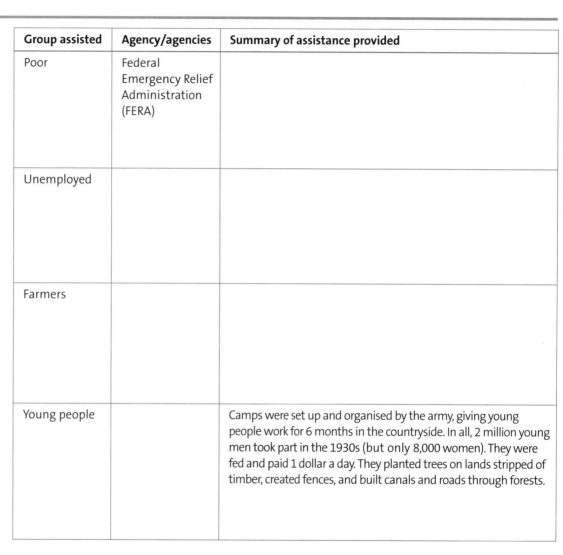

7 Complete the table, which refers to the first 100 days of Roosevelt's presidency.

Group assisted	Agency/agencies	Summary of assistance provided
Poor	Federal Emergency Relief Administration (FERA)	
Unemployed		
Farmers		
Young people		Camps were set up and organised by the army, giving young people work for 6 months in the countryside. In all, 2 million young men took part in the 1930s (but only 8,000 women). They were fed and paid 1 dollar a day. They planted trees on lands stripped of timber, created fences, and built canals and roads through forests.

8 a What were the main aims of the second New Deal?

8a

b Why was it introduced?

b

9 How did the second New Deal help:
a improve the rights of workers?

9a

b the old, unemployed and sick?

b

c the poor people living in rural areas?

c

10 Many artists, actors, writers and photographers were helped by the New Deal. How and why did the federal government provide help for these groups of people?

10

....
....
....
....
....
....

11 Read Source C. Does this source give an accurate view of how the New Deal affected Americans?

11

....
....
....
....
....
....
....
....
....
....
....

Source C

I hate to think what would have happened if this work had not come. I'd sold or traded everything I could. And my kids were hungry. I stood in front of the window of the bakeshop down the street and wondered just how long it would be before I got desperate enough to pick up a rock and heave it through that window and grab some bread to take home.

An ex-businessman in Montana speaking in 1933. He was employed laying sewer pipes, wearing his business suit.

From E. P. Hill, *Franklin Roosevelt and the New Deal*, 1975

Topic 7 Recovery?

This is the second of two topics that consider the nature and impact of Roosevelt's New Deal from 1933 to 1941. This topic examines the opposition to the New Deal, and the extent of the success of the New Deal legislation passed after 1933.

Key question

How successful was the New Deal?

Key content

- Opposition to the New Deal — Republicans, interests of the rich and big business, Supreme Court, and radical critics
- Unemployment and the Depression
- The impact of the Second World War on the US economy

Opposition

 Why did the New Deal encounter opposition?

Never before had any US president sought to establish such control over the economy. The power of the federal government grew during the 1930s, and many came to view Roosevelt as a would-be dictator. To some, Roosevelt's New Deal went too far and they saw him as acting in an 'un-American way'.

However, to others, Roosevelt's policies were not radical enough, and he failed to alleviate the worst effects of the Depression.

Opposition to Roosevelt also emerged from one of the most powerful institutions of USA — the Supreme Court.

Opposition from the Republicans

Republican politicians criticised Roosevelt on three major counts:

- The money spent on relief was often wasteful. For example, the number of American civil servants nearly doubled between 1933 and 1939.
- The approach of the New Deal made Americans too dependent on the state and interfered too much in people's lives, e.g. the regulations and rules in the agencies were too stringent.
- Federal government interfered in the traditional freedoms of business.

Opposition from big business and the rich

The Republican Party was backed by the business leaders who did well in the economic prosperity of the 1920s. Big businesses and rich people soon became critical of the New Deal, especially the second New Deal. Their criticism of Roosevelt became highly personal — he was described as a traitor to his class and a socialist born from a wealthy family.

Richer businessmen felt that Roosevelt's leadership was costing them the freedom to run their own businesses. In particular:

- The development of collective bargaining by more trade unions had strengthened workers' rights.
- They had to pay higher taxes to pay for the government's reforms.

As a result, the Liberty League was founded in 1934. This was supported by millionaire businessmen to defend private wealth and business.

Table 1 Trade union membership in the USA

	1934	1940
Total workforce (millions)	53	56
Total trade union membership (millions)	3.2	8.9
Percentage of workforce in trade unions	6.03	15.9

Radical critics

Roosevelt's success at the elections cannot disguise the fact that many Americans were not satisfied with the New Deal, and some wanted more radical social and economic changes. The most influential opponents were:

- **Senator Huey Long (the Kingfish)** — perhaps Roosevelt's most significant opponent. In 1934, he set up a movement called 'Share Our Wealth', after being disappointed with the New Deal. This was a more radical programme of wealth redistribution that appealed to many Americans. Long proposed to take away the wealth of those with fortunes exceeding $3 million and give sufficient money to every family to allow them to buy a house, car and radio. Old people would gain pensions, there would be a national minimum wage and a shorter working week. In 1935, Long was assassinated, putting an end to the movement.
- **Father Charles Coughlin** — a Canadian Catholic priest who had supported Roosevelt. He broadcasted regularly on the radio, developing a large following, and formed the National Union for Social Justice in 1934. His ideas were anti-communist, anti-trade union — an American version of Italian fascism. In the 1936 presidential election, Coughlin's 'Union' candidate, William Lemke, polled under 1 million votes. Coughlin then moved further to the right, becoming violently anti-Semitic.
- **Dr Francis Townsend** — who appealed to the elderly. He set up 'Old Age Revolving Pensions' in 1934. He proposed to pay each American over the age of 60 a pension of $200 a month, provided those people retired from work and spent their entire pension each month, as a way of increasing spending. The Social Security Act of 1935 left many Americans out of the

The 1936 presidential election

Candidate	Votes (millions)
F. D. Roosevelt (Democrat)	27.2
A. Landon (Republican)	16.8
W. Lemke (Union)	0.8

1936 marked the high point of both Roosevelt's popularity and the New Deal. Roosevelt won the presidential election with 27.2 million votes — 60.5% of all votes. He then went on to win the presidential elections in 1940 and 1944.

After 1936, Roosevelt became more cautious on the economic front, and in 1937 he cut the New Deal budget, triggering increased unemployment. By 1938, the Republicans were performing better in congressional elections than the Democrats.

pension scheme, and these people were attracted to Townsend's organisation. From 1936, financial irregularity caused the organisation to fall apart and Townsend faded from view.

- **Socialists**. Some on the left wing of the political spectrum wanted to go further. They wanted the state to take control of the economy and put an end to private ownership. A few Communists in the USA even supported Stalin's USSR as an alternative model. However, their political support remained limited.

Roosevelt and the Supreme Court

The US Constitution vested great powers in the Supreme Court, which had the power to decide whether Acts passed by Congress were made law. The most serious opposition to Roosevelt came from this body, which in 1935 and 1936 declared 11 of the laws of the New Deal (such as the NRA and the AAA) 'unconstitutional', because they interfered with the rights of the states.

After winning a landslide victory in the 1936 presidential election, Roosevelt asked Congress to pass a new bill reforming the Supreme Court. It had two key features:

- to stop any judge serving beyond the age of 70
- to increase the size of the Court from 9 to 15

Roosevelt's proposals were aimed at countering the political opposition to the New Deal, but they also gave him much more power.

This action provoked widespread alarm. Many people accused Roosevelt of seeking the powers of a dictator, and he was forced to back down. However, shaken by the threats to its

independence, the Supreme Court became more co-operative after 1932, approving the main measures of Roosevelt's second New Deal.

Unemployment and the Depression

 What were the successes and failures of the New Deal?

Unemployment fell steadily from 1933 until 1937, but rose again in the following 2 years when Roosevelt began to limit spending. It was only after 1939 that unemployment fell in a sustained manner, due to the outbreak of war in Europe.

In terms of success, the New Deal brought relief to the unemployed, restored confidence in the US banking system and benefited the American economy in the medium and longer term.

Although Roosevelt won the 1936 presidential election, his New Deal was the subject of much debate, focusing on the extent of its success and whether all Americans benefited from it. The following paragraphs give a brief overview of the successes and failures of the New Deal.

Young Americans

The CCC aimed to give work to unemployed young men, and at its height employed 500,000 men in 200 camps across the USA. It helped them gain employment experience and taught thousands to read and write. However, membership was predominantly white, the work was largely unskilled and at the end of the scheme there was no guaranteed job. As part of the WPA, a separate National Youth Administration was established in 1935. It provided money for young people to go to university and college, helping thousands gain qualifications. It also made an effort to help black Americans.

Farmers

Farmers and farm workers were among the worst off in American society. Although the AAA increased farm incomes from $4.5 billion in 1933 to $6.9 billion in 1935, it mainly helped richer farmers who owned large farms. Some of the poor tenant farmers were forced to leave their farms and migrate.

The Farm Credit Administration helped many farmers keep their farms by providing loans. The TVA brought major improvements to that area, but the Resettlement Act of 1935 failed on the whole and thousands of farmers and labourers from states such as Oklahoma and Arkansas fled the 'dust bowl'. They travelled to California, often receiving a hostile reception upon their arrival.

Black Americans

Black Americans continued to be disadvantaged, making little progress towards civil rights. Roosevelt was dependent on the support of white Democrats in the South, the laws of the New Deal allowed black workers to be paid less than white ones, and many poor black farmers lost their land in the 1930s. However, a lot of black Americans gained jobs through the CCC and other agencies, and some benefited from house-building projects. In 1941, Roosevelt passed an order that banned racial discrimination in defence industries, helping thousands of black Americans to gain employment during the Second World War.

Native Americans

In 1934, the Indian Reorganisation Act safeguarded Native American culture for the first time. Tribes were reorganised into self-governing bodies, were able to pass their own laws and set up their own police and governments. However, by 1941 the economic position of Native Americans had changed little and most remained poor.

Women

Women made little progress towards equality — they were still paid less than men for the same work. However, more women entered professional jobs through the creation of a Women's and Professional Division of the WPA, and First Lady Eleanor Roosevelt did much to aid the advancement of women.

Industrial workers

Many industrial workers benefited from the new jobs created, the strengthening of workers' rights through the NRA and the measures of the second New Deal. However, despite the growing power of the union movement, many strikes were broken up violently and companies often employed their own thugs for this purpose.

The Second World War and economic recovery

 How did the Second World War affect the US economy?

Although the New Deal brought relief to millions of unemployed Americans and introduced other benefits, there is no doubt that the outbreak of war in Europe in 1939 brought about full economic recovery in the USA. Roosevelt acknowledged this when he said: 'Doctor New Deal stopped the patient from dying. Doctor Second World War brought about economy recovery.'

The Second World War

Germany's invasion of Poland in September 1939 led to the outbreak of war in Europe. The American people were generally loath to join Britain and France because isolationism was still strong, so Roosevelt kept the USA neutral.

It was not until Japan attacked the US navy at Pearl Harbor on 7 December 1941 that the USA joined the Allies against the fascist powers of Germany, Italy and Japan.

Before US industrial production soared in 1938, the unemployment rate was 19%. By 1940 it was 14.6% and by 1942 it was 4.7%. Farmers prospered with a guaranteed market, big business increased its profits through huge orders from the government, and the older industries (coal, iron, steel, oil and shipbuilding) were boosted by the demands of the war. Consumer industries also did well and national income grew, as did individual personal wealth.

🔑 Key question

How successful was the New Deal?

Aims of the New Deal

- To restore confidence in the banking system, thereby encouraging Americans to save
- To help industry, business and farming to recover
- To cut unemployment
- To provide relief to those who were hit hardest by the Depression

Successes

- Restoration of confidence in the banking system
- Provision of relief to those most in need
- Creation of jobs for many of the unemployed
- Improved welfare provision
- Enhancement of the rights of workers

Failures

- Unemployment remained very high, and rose after 1937.
- Benefits for women, native and black Americans were limited.
- Many were left out of the welfare provisions.

Conclusion

- The New Deal achieved much economically and socially.
- Roosevelt's political success, winning four presidential elections, is testament to his popular support, despite his political opposition.
- Nevertheless, the extent of America's problems in the early 1930s were enormous, and there were significant limitations and weaknesses to the New Deal.
- The USA did not achieve full economic recovery until the outbreak of war in Europe in 1939.

Figure 1 How successful was the New Deal?

Questions

Use the information on pages 68–72, your class notes and textbooks to answer the following questions.

1 Who opposed the New Deal and why? Complete the table to answer this question. Continue on a separate sheet if necessary.

Opponents of the New Deal	Was opposition due to the New Deal doing too much or too little?	Summary of opposition
Republicans		
	Too much	
		He proposed to pay each American over the age of 60 a pension of $200 a month, provided those people retired.

2 Study Source A.

a What is the message of this cartoon?

b Was this cartoon drawn by an opponent or a supporter of the New Deal?

c How useful is this cartoon to a historian studying American attitudes towards the New Deal in 1933? Consider both the usefulness and the limitations of the cartoon.

2a

b

c

Source A

Questions

Source B

A resident of Park Avenue, an area of New York where the rich live, was recently sent to prison for threatening violence to President Roosevelt. This shows the fanatical hatred of the President which today obsesses thousands of men and women among the upper class.

From 'They Hate Roosevelt', an article published in 1936

3 Read Source B. Explain why some Americans hated Roosevelt and his New Deal. Use the source and your own knowledge to explain your answer.

3

4 a How and why did the US Supreme Court oppose the New Deal?

4a

b How did Roosevelt attempt to overcome opposition from the Supreme Court?

b

5 a Using the graph in Figure 1,
explain why unemployment:
- fell after 1933
- rose after 1937
- fell after 1939

b Do the data in Figure 1 prove that
the New Deal was a failure?

5a

....

....

....

....

....

b

....

....

....

....

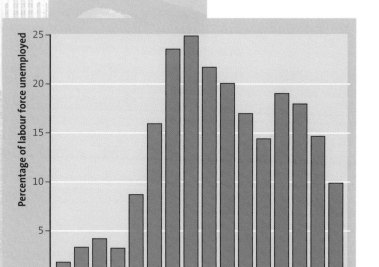

Figure 1

....

....

....

....

....

....

....

Questions

6 Complete the table to explain how the New Deal affected American society in the 1930s.

Social group	Benefits from the New Deal	Limitations of the New Deal
Businessmen		
The unemployed	Gained jobs through the various agencies created, such as the PWA.	
The poor, elderly and sick		
Industrial workers		
The young		
Farmers		
Women		
Native Americans		Most remained very poor and were excluded from American society.
Black Americans		

Source C

The main reason for our economic recovery was the spending of government money on public works, work relief, and agricultural adjustment and resettlement programmes.

Frances Perkins, Secretary of Labor in Roosevelt's government, *The Roosevelt I Knew*, 1947

7 Read Sources C and D.

  a How do the content of Sources C and D differ?

  b Explain possible reasons why these two interpretations are different.

Source D

During Franklin Roosevelt's first term, the New Deal did not cure the underlying economic problems. It was the war that did that. Within a matter of months, 6 million workers found new jobs. Within a couple of years, mass unemployment had virtually disappeared.

G. Hodgson, *In Our Time*, 1976

7a

b

8 Read Source E. Is this an accurate interpretation of the achievements of the New Deal?

Source E

The basic goals of President Roosevelt were relief, recovery and reform. The New Deal's greatest success was in the area of relief. Employing a bewildering number of alphabet agencies, the government brought relief to most of the destitute and poor. Yet not everyone was taken care of.

D. R. McCoy, *Coming of Age: America during the 1920s and 1930s*, 1973

8

Extended writing

On separate paper, write a short essay in answer to the following question.

9 Was the New Deal a success or a failure?

Complete the planning grid opposite to help you answer this question, giving examples where possible.

9

Aims of the New Deal	
Successes of the New Deal	
Failures/limitations of the New Deal	
Conclusion	